Life is a Journey
Happy Traveling

Mary Boyer

POEMS AND
REFLECTIONS

Mary Boyer

ORIGINAL WRITING

ISBN: 978-1-907179-22-8

A CIP catalogue for this book is available from the National Library.

Published by Original Writing Ltd., Dublin, 2009.

Printed in Great Britain by the MPG Books Group, Bodmin and King's Lynn

Acknowledgements

I would like to thank Dillon for his support, patience and all the photographs he took for my book, the front and back cover, my parents and myself.

My son Michael for his inspiration and encouragement.

Grateful thanks to Kathleen Griffin for typing and copying my manuscript onto disc. Also to her father Tim Griffin for his encouragement.

To Sean Quinlan P.C. for putting my Foreword together.

Special thanks to Barty for his loyal friendship and gift.

To all my family and friends for their support

Dedicated to the memory of my parents.

Foreword

The great Irish poet Thomas Davis once wrote that poetry
'Arouses the deepest passion in us.
It binds us to the land by its condensed and gem-like history, and
to the future by examples and asperations.
It fires us in action and sheds a grace around our homes.'

Marys new book of poems and reflections does all these things.
It is a valuable contribution to the literature of Kerry.
It speaks from the heart rekindling memories of laughter and
tears. I wish her every success in this new venture, and trust we
will hear more of Marys poems and reflections in the future,
which both educate and entertain.

Sean Quinlan P.C.

Contents

POEMS AND
REFLECTIONS

Blushing borders

One pleasant morning in early June,
I seen a host of flowers,
They were every colour hue,
The sun-shine and the showers,
Was all they needed plus morning dew,
Late spring puts the Winter flowers to bed,
The climbers head skywards,
On the trellis and the shed,

June roses bloom, in every colour red,
Then come late tulips,
They spring from their earthly bed,
In May the bluebells make their mark,
And round about the meadows you can hear a lark,
Early summer has arrived,
And with her warmth we will feel revived.

Woodland flowers

I walked through the wood,
The wild honeysuckle was in bud,
I knew it was too early in the year
To pick and smell that lovely scent,
It will bloom I know, I have no fear,
From Heaven only could that wild flower be sent.

In May at the dawn of day
The bluebells are a sight to be seen,
With their dresses of blue and green,
Nodding like bells, in the morning dew
Waiting for the sun to shine on them and you.

It would lift your spirits high to see,
If I was there alone, for hours on end,
It would not be long enough for me
The wind has a special sound
So all of nature gathers round.

The leaves, trees and all the wild flowers, have a party
They all play games, the wind provides the music,
You can hear them laugh hail and hearty,
And all is happy 'til the midnight hour,
When all will sleep in that happy bower.

The early Spring

We are all glad to see the end of Winter,
She can take her wind, snow and rain,
As after the Winter months we are drained,
January appears, and for us a new year.

The snow-drops are such pretty flowers,
They always seem to survive the heaviest showers,
Jack Frost won't do them any harm,
And the earth round them keeps them warm,
They are nodding their heads,
Bleary-eyed not long out of bed,
I think they lie in wait for Spring to show,
And wonder why Winter went so slow.

Snow-drops look so sweet,
They bloom in out-of-way places,
Trying to look discreet,
It's all they can do to stop their dancing feet,
They dress in white and green,
We look and say where have you been?
It's been a long year,
And they say in return, "Have no fear,
We were only sleeping,
While you were getting on with your lives,
We were peeping."

THE MOUNTAINS IN WINTER

Today I sat and watched the mountains,
So much life, clouds of grey, black and gold,
Snow-capped, looked so cold.

Yet they changed colour before my eyes,
I've seen shades of green, purple and blue
And then the sun shone and turned the mountains into a heavenly blue.

I am convinced something greater than us
Is at work constantly,
To surprise and amaze, not creating any fuss.

When you watch the mountains,
You get carried away
On a flight of fancy
Where you want to stay.

High above the plains and lowlands,
Where we could pray and to God raise our hands,
What I am writing is true,
All the beauty is waiting for you.

And of course I can always put my mind on a flight of fancy,
There is no limit as I soar,
The range my mind's eye can see more and more.

14/11/08

Winter is at an end

Now that Winter is at an end
She can put away her robes of snow and frost,
The earth will have the chance to mend
And make up for time lost.

To look at the silver lake and dream
See the wildlife enjoy the sun,
Watch new leaves and flowers
Look at their reflection in the stream.

The drowsy cuckoo and the sleeping bee
I will listen for the cuckoo's call,
Soon we will have April showers,
But first we must have March.

Who can roar like a lion
And her winds can bite
Until the sun gives her warmth and light,
We can hear the birds begin to sing
They are glad we will soon have Spring.

Winter Roads

Enjoy the cold
A new year is waiting to unfold,
A season diminishes and ceases,
Another takes its place and increases.

Winter trees are empty of their leaves,
Between the thin branches the cold wind blows,
Before too long the children get their wish,
As from the North the winds bring snow.

The night is a dark boudoir,
Bestowing to stars 'til the dawn hour,
The long Winter night can give an enviable peace,
As nature is resting and taking her ease.

This time of year we like to gather near,
So we can feel close to ones so dear,
We celebrate Christmas and New Year,
And raise our glasses full of good cheer.

Soon the snowdrops will peep through,
It seems, with their nodding heads
They are saying, "How do you do?"
They have been sleeping in their earthly beds

Snowdrops can make the darkest day seem bright,
We all love to see such a beautiful sight
There they are nodding in their coast of green and white.

The magic of snow

We did not expect it to snow,
But we were so glad,
To school we could not go,
It sounded quiet and all around was white,
The sky looked so clear,
And the sun shone so bright,
We played snow-balls from morn till night,
Icicles did hang in every colour hue,
All the earth looked new,
The snow lay thick on the eaves,
And then the sun made the snow melt,
And warmed the frosted leaves,
The children built snowmen,
And there were lots of snow-balls threw,
But, the sun in a short while,
Melts the snow and ice, with her smile,
For she knows we need her warmth to survive,
Not just us, but every thing that's alive,
So on her way, the snow hurries,
With help from the north wind,
She takes off in a flurry,
But as always will appear,
During the Winter of each year.

Winter

Winter has arrived when we draw the curtains and cosy up warm,
The year is coming to an end,
And has done us no harm.

So we will celebrate Christmas and all the festive theme,
The food, wine, sweets and all that Christmas means.

But we must not forget the Baby who was born in a stall,
So many, many years ago, let's not forget at all.

The 'New Year' will appear all shiny and new,
So let's hope the 'New Year' is good for me and you.

We are always planning for whatever,
Let's enjoy the now and not worry about tomorrow,
For life is short and bitter sweet,
So we will do the best we can
Before our Maker we meet.

New Year will lead to Spring,
From Winter on the year will go,
I feel sure we will have some snow before the Winter is out,
Then we can play snowballs out and about.

01/10/08

MY AUTUMN NEARING WINTER

I now realise that I have lived seventy years,
And lived a lot, some joy some tears,
But that's how life is and always will be.

For each of us are so unique,
You and me are so different, but of the same,
I'm your Mum and we share the same name.

When I think of Winter-time of my life,
I wonder what life brings, perhaps strife.

I enjoyed my Spring and Summer time,
And am grateful for my life,
I got to be a mother and a wife,
Life is short but sweet,
So let's arrange a time to meet.

06/10/08

21/12/2008 -The shortest day

At sunrise today,
The sun was slow to get up,
As though she was saying, "Go fill up my cup,
For today I have only a few hours to shine,
As this is the shortest day of the year,
I will do my best to put a smile on your face",
The hours are short, but we will win the race,
As each year repeats, we have been here before,
And hopefully we will see many more.

Soon it will be Christmas tide,
And we will celebrate worldwide,
Perhaps spread a little joy,
And remember that little boy,
Who so long ago gave us light,
To see the crib, and the stars shining bright,
All the birds are seeking their nests,
It's now getting dusk,
And our sun will soon take her rest.

But tomorrow is another day,
We will ask God to let us stay,
Life is good, there should be no need to push,
As many times over we get caught up in the rush,
In six month's time, it will be Summer,
And we will look back at Winter in slumber,
But at present Summer is hidden out of sight,
And not ours to plan or plith.

The fading light 2008

I walked on the beach and watched the fading light of 2008,
Another year closing, not long to wait
For the new year to unfold,
The sea was calm, the sky looked cold,
But then I expected that, as our year was twelve months old.

The waves seemed out of reach,
But near enough to hear their lapping on the beach,
As the New Year starts, we will be given another chance
Maybe to mend old scores and relationships to enhance.

The light is nearly gone as we put another year behind us,
I see a new moon and Venus the star of love,
The moon promises hope and shines upon us from above.

The clouds seem to be in a hurry,
The wind is from the North, we might get a snow flurry,
As the last ray of sunlight shines on the sea
I feel she is waving to you and me,
So we look forward to a new day,
As Old Master Time waits for no one and ticks away.

21/12/08

Each new day

When I awake, I always say thank God for another day,
Another chance to start anew,
And in my dreams I dreamt of you,
Always glad I am alive and well,
I am always amazed and never fazed
On the wonders of the world, in which I dwell,
As on our way we go,
Through our acts, we will leave some tracks,
Like footprints in the snow,
So choose how you will live today,
Fill every minute, and every hour,
And make the day go slow.

Live for today

Live for today and enjoy each hour,
The sun, the moon each tree and flower,
Be thankful for all the little things,
That into our hearts such happiness brings.

For we cannot choose the day,
When God will call us away,
So make the most of what you possess,
Remember you cannot buy happiness,
It rests with each one of us every day,
To pass on a smile as we go on our way,
For tomorrow we may be gone.

A PERFECT DAY

The rain has moved on
And left a new day,
Nothing seems to move everything is still
It's just another perfect day.

The shadows and light
That move with the wind,
Hidden violets grow
Splashed with summer spray.

Just another perfect day,
On the wild and misty hillside,
Fear is nature's warning
Hunger is never far away.

And all of this world is for
Children that play,
Days that never end
Always should remain.

IMAGINATION

First of all this picture says a lot,
The sky meeting the mountains,
Then the mountains meeting the ground,
I think they're saying, "Look at me, I am waiting to
Be explored" a climb or walk, taking in the view,
Stopping here and there to survey, the beauty 'round us.

I see stepping stones on the foreshore,
To entice us to try and walk out, a challenge I suppose,
To see how far we can go before the water gets deep,
So there are always boundaries, in all paths in life.

They are there to help us survive,
A barrier between us and danger,
Then the beautiful reflection on the water,
Like we see when we look in the mirror,
Only we never see ourselves as others see us,
It has the right title, "Stillness" it says, look I am still, tranquil,
in reflective mood,
In my mind I am wondering has the sun gone to rest,
Or is she rising, to greet a new day, I am not sure,
But I will expect that, at present, she is out of sight,
Content to give her light,
It's true every picture tells a story.

It came over the hill

A summer storm is a wondrous thing to behold,
See how it brews and then how it unfold,
It starts with a breeze so gentle on your back,
Then it lights up the sky with its lightening track,
Hear the distant thunder as clouds part and sever,
Soon the sky will be purple just like mountain heather,
Roaring in now the wind bending the trees,
Enough to bring mature oaks down to their knees,
No mercy is given as the storm takes its course,
You can only wonder at its majesty as it shouts 'til it's hoarse,
And then the quietness all around,
Only the drip, drip, drip from leaves comes the sound,
Of raindrops finding their way back to earth,
The ground drinks up greedily as it touches the turf,
And finally hush and lovely fresh road smell,
The only reminder of the storm that all at once did yell.

WILD FANCY ROAMS AFAR

As idly flits the willow wren from tree to tree
Wild fancy likes to soar, with no care
Like a fettered spirit, trying to break free
You can see her upward soar on the trembling air,
As the sunlight the shaded nooks do fill
With a reflected glow,
While all her world stands still
She sees an opening in the azure sky
Where a maze of cloudlets flow,
The thrill of light, joy and power
Takes wild fancy to her happy bower.

Fancy

For ever let the fancy roam,
Pleasure is never found at home,
At a touch sweet pleasure melteth
Just like a bubble when the rain pelteth.

Then let winged fancy wonder,
Open up the cage door,
And watch her as she skywards soars,
Like an eagle as she ponders.

Sweet, sweet Fancy let her loose,
Summer's joys are spoilt by use,
As the enjoying of spring,
Just fades away like her blossoming.

When the night does meet the moon,
It will be like the sun shines at high noon,
Fancy high commissioned send her,
She will bring it all together,
All the delights of summer weather.

The bluebells, primroses and buds of May,
From a dewy grass or the smell of new mown hay,
Fancy will bring in spite of frost,
So many lovely things we thought were lost.

And every leaf and every flower,
Washed from the self-same shower,
We will see the field-mouse peep,
Ready for another spring, after his long sleep.

Oh sweet Fancy let her loose,
Everything is spoilt by use,
Where is the cheek that does not fade,
And that lovely smile that now is in shade.

Then let Fancy find,
A mistress for your mind,
Of Fancy's string and mesh,
Let her break free, let her off her leash.

If you listen you will hear,
Church bells ringing out so clear,
I think they're saying Spring is on its way,
And we can thank God for another day.

All the birds are singing,
And to build their nests they're bringing
Feathers, wool, sticks and straw,
You can hear the rooks with their loud caw.

So let Fancy roam,
Break her prison string,
And such joys as these she'll bring,
Set her free, let her roam,
Pleasure never is at home.

The joy of giving

They say a thing of beauty is a joy for ever,
Its loveliness never ceases,
You would say quite bower, for us to sleep,
To watch the sun rise as she peeps,
And in Spring, an April shower,
To refresh the leaves and flowers,

A thing of beauty will not distain,
Even on the gloomiest day, it will remain,
What beauty in Spring,
To hear the birds sing,
To watch the lambs play,
We are given such wonderful things,
It would make you want to pray,

Of all the seasons of the year,
The look and smell of Spring,
When she appears,
After the long Winter, she tries to reason,
The trees get new leaves and blossom,
Oh the joy of baby lambs,
You want to hold them to your bosom.

Trees old and young, sprouting a coat of green,

The apple and cherry blossom,

Have to be seen,

Half way through the year, we meet the month of June,

Even that gold light we call the moon,

Does have competition,

When we see her roses in bloom,

A thing of beauty is a joy for ever,

Its loveliness ceasing never.

School days

School days for me I did dread,
I would be planning all the way,
How would I not have to go,
With every step I tread.
When the sun was shining, I'd be thinking,
What I could do with the day,
Perhaps walk in the fields, admire the wild flowers,
Even sit fishing for minnows,
With a jam jar at the ready for my catch,
But they would swim by in a flash.

When you think, how can a bird that is born to fly,
Have to sit in a cage, and not wish to die,
Any one would go in a rage,
Oh to go to school on a summer morn,
It would drive all joy away,
I had a good imagination,
A gift I was given when I was born,
I could escape all the books,
As out the window I looked.

Ah then at times I did sit and stare,
Into a land beyond all care,
For I knew after school there would be no holding
Me, no more rules.
They say schooldays should be your happiest days,
Where that saying came from I don't like to think,

As my memories of those years for me still stink.
In my books I could take no delight,
And on my life school put a blight,
I feel now I was robbed of all that special time,
When I should have been happy and gay,
But we can't turn back the clock, so they say,
It's true if buds are nipped,
And blossom blown away,
No tender plants should be stripped,
Of joy, in their blooming day.

Time

They say when God made time, he made plenty of it
Time it is a precious thing, make no mistake about it,
It flits away in the blink of an eye,
And never returns no matter how we try,
When I was young there was so much to do,
Searching in hedgerows for birds nests,
I had to, just had to, swing on a five bar gate,
My mother would be angry, because I was always late,
I always took my time to school,
Needless to say I broke the golden rule,
I always loved to climb a tree,
Up to the top I would go,
And if I fell I would not let it show,
I was always late for dinner,
And never on time for tea,
But that was a special time
Oh, to bring it all back
We picked horse-chestnuts,
Then we used our shoe-laces to play hic-hack,
So in my mind I can see the bird's nests,
The gate I swung on
The tree that grew so tall,
No matter how I call,
Old Master Time says, no turning back,
On and go and be careful you don't fall.

Back to yesterday

A fluttering of swallow's tails
Upon the air they play,
A glimpse of honeysuckle
And the smell of new-mown hay,
The hawthorn is in full bloom, so bright
When the breeze blows, covering the ground white.

The gentle air to greet,
I stroll beneath
My yesterday's to meet,
To touch the cold and earthy soil,
I hasten there to tread on
To see these scenes once more I pray
No price I will have to pay.

The lane-way twisting calm and green,
In my memory, I'm sure it's to heaven I've been,
I just close my eyes to the bright, bright skies
And walk back to yesterday.

8/1/09

The best things in life are free

When we were young, we had few treats,
If we got cake or sweets,
We had a smile on our face for weeks,
Always the small things gave us joy,
Christmas and birthdays, we might get a toy.

After Winter, oh how we welcomed Spring,
When we could play outside, loud the birds did sing,
In Spring seen the daffodils,
And in the hedge the primroses grew,
The bluebells were such a beautiful hue,
We ran and we raced, and chased each other up the hills,
By the time bedtime came, we had had our fill.

We had a picnic in the Summer time,
The sweet smell of new mown hay,
All such simple fun,
We wished it would last for ever and a day,
So Summer slipped away,
And Autumn started to wear her red and gold dresses,
I think she was out to impress,
Autumn likes the golden leaves,
And wears red berries in her tresses,
The wind blows strong all 'round,
We try and put the leaves in a mound,
Then the wind swirls and wherls,
And blows the leaves 'round,

We used to kick and shuffle them into a pile,
After that we would have a race and run a mile.

The Winter days drew near,
And every thing seemed to dull and drear,
The birds have flown to warmer climes,
Soon it will be Christmas,
And we will hear the church bells chime,
But holly and red berries,
Help to bring a little cheer,
Then we will celebrate New Year.

The Sea

I went one morning with my dog,
And walked along the beach,
The tide was out and so I thought,
That we were out of reach.

But as we walked, to my surprise,
The sea had caught our heels and eyes,
She is always restless and never still,
Perhaps she's angry and has a strong will.

In the evening at close of day,
The sun shines on her in a special way,
As though she is saying have a quiet night,
And I will see you in the morning light.

We must respect her and watch her waves,
As she can be rough and temperamental,
Many a life she was taken when badly she behaved,
So enjoy the sea and treat her gentle.

There is a story, you can hear the sea through a shell,
If you hold it to your ear,
Perhaps she has secrets she will not tell,
I am sure the sea has many stories,
If we listen we can hear.

Lovers like to spend time romancing,
And find the beach ideal for dancing
I could spend all day and night waiting for her waves,
She is very loyal, always there to listen to my raves.

So now I will bid her goodnight,
And dream of the time I will see her in sunlight.

18/10/08

A lone boat

I see a loan boat at water's edge,
Is it arriving or leaving,
The sea-gulls are flying above,
Perhaps they think there is a fish on board,
The sea looks calm and all is quiet,
Maybe the little boat has travelled through the night.

It's all very calming, only the water lapping gently on the shore,
A light blue sky above,
With the promise of a new day.

The sand has no footprints,
So it makes me think,
Where is the person that arrived on the small boat.
Are they still sitting, watching the view,
Or are they planning their next adventure?
I feel they will return and leave as they arrived alone,
Yet content, as they have all they need,
Their dreams, time, the sea, sky, sun, moon and stars,
And all that Heaven allows,
So now I will bid them a safe journey,
Farewell adieu.

The seagull

A lonely seagull flies the winds,
Majestic – soaring – gliding wings,
A single flight with me
Come here and fly with me, and show me how it feels to be free.

My spirit floats to be a part,
I feel the beating of its heart,
My soul, one with the bird of sea
Now knows the feeling to be free.

I feel the winds caress my soul,
And soar the streams without a goal,
My being trembles of delight
A treasure I received tonight.

The seagull's flight of soaring high,
The gift of what it means to fly.

27/12/08

MICHAEL'S POEM

I think I can now see the land,
Never guessed or could have planned,
But journey's nearing its end,
And the sail is bellowing, and on the mend.

Feel no more the need to walk the past,
Got a feeling now my die is cast,
I had to learn, but now I can see,
It was always there in front of me.

My footsteps were hidden in the fog,
But now the wind has cleared the smog,
I have been in the dark too long
Now it's time to sing my song.

My reply

I can see clearly now the rain has gone,
Sometimes the clouds can block the sun,
Then when the rain-clouds clear away,
We can see for ever and a day,
But we will not worry if we have to wait
For all the storm clouds to clear,
As you have found a new door and gate,
And it will all be worth it,
Even if you have to wait.

But at present, and that's all we have,
You can spend time looking and searching,
For all your heart's desires,
Be it dreaming, screaming or just looking for a moon-beam,
The sky's the limit, and you have your dreams,
Not a bad place to be, as we look at life and see things,
In other words, we are like eagles with wings.

Your footsteps I feel will lead you on,
Now the fog and the smog has gone,
The things that clouded your view,
Have now melted like morning dew,
I would say there is no need to linger,
As you and only you hold the string on your finger.

As for two rambling roses that's fine,
But remember they both grow separately,
And don't always have to be entwined,
Because like you and me,
If we were to close to any one or any thing,
We would have to have space, or we would break free.

Two years later

Has no one said those daring, kind eyes should be more learned,
Or warned you how despairing the moths are when they are burned?
I could have warned you but you were young,
So we speak with a different tongue.

O you will take whatever is offered,
And dream that all the world's a friend,
Suffer as your mother suffered,
Be as broken in the end,
But I am old and you are young,
And so I speak with a different tongue.

A NEW START

It has come as no surprise,
That someone has opened your eyes,
To all that is beautiful around,
But you must keep both feet on the ground.

So you can fly with the wings of a dove,
For us all life is so fragile,
There are so many ways to love,
We must dance, sing and smile.

Life is full of ups-and-downs,
It's not what happens to us,
Remember it's how we cope that counts,
You see at one time you thought you had problems
you could not surmount.

I have watched and listened to you growing strong,
Just reading between the lines,
I knew you could not go wrong.

And now you can nearly touch the sky,
All this and more in your hands,
You have seen the glow that catches your eye.

Who knows? In future you will be able to give
Some lost soul the will to live,
You will comfort and pleasure,
And knowing you it will be in no small measure.

I must say to end,
You have helped me to mend,
For I was a lost soul until at last,
I put my heart in the future and my torments in the past.

A LIGHT OF FLAMES

I can see the flames lighting the room,
Pushing into corners any leftover gloom,
But none here now my heart is alive,
Can feel its beat and its strong drive,
See those logs roaring awat,
Reminds me of another great day.
And another log and on she goes,
See her spark and feel her glow,
Fire will never end inside my body now,
I know how to feed, I understand my need,
And yours too I feel the spark,
Keep on with life and never ever park,
Embers low now, but know can light,
Only takes a little to burn all night,
So feed the flames, keep those dreams,
And never ever give up the fight,
For what you know is right.

DEAD LOVE

Oh never weep for love that's dead,
Since love is seldom true,
But changes his fashion from blue to red,
From brightest red to blue,
And all love was born to an early death,
And so is seldom true.

Then harbour no smile on your bony face,
To win the deepest sigh,
The fairest words on truest lips,
Pass on and surely die,
And you will stand alone my dear,
When Wintry winds draw nigh.

After love

There is no magic any more,
We meet as other people do,
You work no miracle for me, or I for you,
There is no splendour any more,
I have grown listless as the pool beside the shore,
But though the pool is safe from storm,
The sun does not shine to keep me warm,
Though the water from the pool, the tide releases,
It grows more bitter than the sea, for all its peace.

Wish you were here

As I walked on my own,
The sea looked so green,
The sun shone from a sky of blue,
I thought how nice it would be if I were with you.

We used to share so very much,
Walks, picnics, watching the stars,
We would dance, sing, talk of everything
From the earth to the planet Mars.

I sat under a green palm
And watched the sun play shadows on the sand,
I remembered how once you held my hand,
From that memory of long ago
I got a beautiful feeling of calm.

You were on my mind a lot today,
Perhaps there was a lot I did not say,
Looking back on our lives
There was a time when I loved you so
I would have died if you had to go.

So who knows what the future will bring
Perhaps one day, once more, our hearts will sing,
How wonderful it would be
If we could make a new start,
Maybe we would be able, our hearts to entwine,

All the hours in the day and night would be divine
And we could be as before we drifted apart.

As the sun sets on each day
Before I go to sleep,
I close my eyes, for you I pray
That along life's way
God will you safely keep.

16/1/09

Missing you

The sea rocks have a green moss
The pine needles have red berries,
And I have memories of you,
Speak to me how you miss me,
Tell me how the hours go slow,
I know hours that are more empty,
Than a beggar's cup on a rainy day.

Tell me of how you remember, of how close we once were,
All them happy times must have left their mark,
As for me, they were and always will be,
A large part of my life and heart,
I pray each night, before I sleep,
That you, your angel will safely keep,
For one day in the next world, who knows,
I will meet you, and tell you I missed you so.

It seems sometimes like yesterday,
Handing over to today,
Like sunshine on water, and surf shining gold,
I felt I had to write this story to be told,
Ours was a special love,
No other before or since, how could there be,
When I was made for you and you for me?

How sad it seems

Sweet, there is nothing left to say, but this,
That love is never lost,
Keen Winter stabs the breast of May,
Whose crimson rose burnt his frost,
Ships tempest tossed,
Will find a harbour in some bay,
And so we may,
And there is nothing left to do,
But to kiss once again and part,
Nay there is nothing we should rue,
I have my beauty, you your art,
Nay do not start, one word was not enough for two,
Like me and you.

Her voice

The wild bee reels from bough to bough,
With his furry coat and gauzy wing,
Now in a lily cup, and now setting a silent bell to swing,
Sit closer love, it was here you and I made that vow,
Sincere that two lives would become as one
As long as the seagull loved the sea,
As long as the sun-flower sought the sun,
It will be for eternity, put your trust in you and me.

Dear friend those times are over and done,
Love's web is spun,
Look upward where the poplar trees,
Sway and sway in the Summer breeze,
Here in the valley never a breeze,
Scatters the thistledown,
But there, great winds blow fair from the
Mighty, mystical seas,
And the wave-lashed lees,
Look upward to where the white gull screams,
What does he see, that we do not see,
Is that a star or a light that gleams,
On some outward argosy?
Ah, can it be,
We have lived our lives in a land of dreams?

GOOD BYE

The flowers of May once welcomed me,
A young girl spoke of love, which was quite natural,
As we were very much in love,
The stars in heaven were dancing with delight,
Now all is bleak, the pathway covered in snow,
I feel the time has come when I must go,
I will have to find my way in the darkness.

With only the moon to guide me on my way,
Love likes to wonder from one to another,
As if God willed that way,
My darling, farewell, I will close the door carefully,
So as not to disturb you in your sleep,
I will write just two words in the snow,
"Good Bye". There is no need to weep.

MOTHER'S WAY

You treasure those things,
Keep them safe in your heart,
Where did the years go?

Everything still so fresh . . . .
The birth, those moments alone,
Your first looking
Into each other's love.

And the visitors
With their wonder and wisdom,
With their gifts and their gazing,
Everything still so fresh . . . .

Then the growing years,
Baby into boy,
Into man,
Into joys and sorrows,
Into life away from your helping
Yet you alone hold his history in your head.

You treasure those things,
Keep them safe in your heart,
Of course you do . . . .

You are his mother.

Memories

I have a box full of memories,
Some happy, some sad,
Some joyful, some bad,
When I grow old, they may grow old with me
And become faded, or they may stay young,
Maybe when I speak of them I will speak in another tongue,

Teasing me as I chase them around my mind,
Trying to catch them but some may decide to leave,
Many more will enter
So for the ones that leave I will not peeve.

But I shall always leave it open,
So that I can take a peek,
And treasure for those few moments
The one I can only find when I go to sleep.

8/1/09

Familiar forgotten

Somehow familiar forgotten,
The brightness of the grass,
And the lush colour of the flowers,
Red and orange,
I walk with you carrying your spirit,
Cradled in my arms, I feel things for you, through you,
Your spirit teaches me its value,
I feel your peace, your contentment,
I look at things as though I had never seen them before,
But they echo something lost, hidden, put aside,
Until a later day,
This day has come I feel,
Each breath is counted, each step,
We walk together, each to each measuring time.

FAMILY PICNIC

Sun's out,

Beautiful about,

Blankets spread,

Papers read,

Sarnies ate,

Got lovely cake,

What a noise

Look at those boys,

Sun going down

Night all still

Kids asleep

Had their fill

Listen now

Breathing calm

Feathers and treasures

Held in their arms

Pick up the bits

Home we go

Want the journey to go slow

Live on the beach

If I had my way

I'd enjoy the sea every day.

1/9/08

My Mother's anniversary

It does not take a special date,
To remember you,
Fifteen years have passed,
Every hour and minute, we miss you so.

Little did we think you would pass away so fast,
I guess your time had come to go,
And God called you home,
It broke our hearts from you to part,
On the day we had to leave you alone.

We never got the chance to say goodbye,
To hold your hand, and kiss you before you closed your eyes,
But I am sure you knew how much we cared,
As you went on your journey to the stars.

I bet you have met all your friends,
And have found Daddy once again,
You had happy times as well as sad,
That's how it is, we had to take the good with the bad.

I know you were tired of pain,
Now all your pain has gone,
Our loss was your gain,
I like to think of you at peace,
Resting and taking your ease,
So now I will let you go,

As knowing you there will be things,
You need to see and do,

Two tired eyes are sleeping,
Two willing hands are still,
She worked so hard for all of us,
Now she is resting at God's will.

25/1/09

The twilight hour

The day is coming to an end,
And evening colours spread
The sun is slowly setting
And the sky is glowing red,
The evening colours,
Enfold the old church tower,
In one last embrace of sunlight,
It is the twilight hour.
The birds that sing at evening
Have such beauty and such power,
They gather 'round and flit and sweep,
Before they find a place to sleep
By now there is but a shadow of the tower,
For all of us 'tis the twilight hour,
And so the earth is pausing,
To hover like a dream world,
In a purple sky,
You cannot deny the magic of the night,

And soon, the moon and stars
Will brighten up our path, with their light.
So one last beam of moonlight,
As we greet the morning star,
A new day begins, and God is watching from afar,
So we will give thanks for the new day,
As at evening, the morning has its power,
Maybe that's why we call it the twilight hour.

Night

At the close of day, before I sleep,
I look through the curtains for one last peep,
I see the stars shining bright
All is well in Heaven tonight.

All alone beside the streams,
I have all night to fulfill my dreams,
Throughout the day, with my friends I stay,
But come night I like to trod,
Far, far away to the land of nod.

The birds too are sleeping in their nests,
And I too must seek mine,
The dew is on the grass,
Spiders are weaving their webs so fine.

If the night sees any weeping,
By those that should have been sleeping,
He will pour sleep on their heads,
And sit down by their beds.

But no matter how hard I try to find the way,
I am never able to get back by day,
Nor can I remember the music and the cheer,
And all those I met, love and hold dear,
For all that belongs to the night,
And God watches over us, not far from sight.

The stars

"Twinkle, twinkle little star,
How I wonder what you are,"
So goes the nursery rhyme
You were here before our time.

There are so many of you,
All with a different hue,
Sometimes hiding from view,
You use the clouds to hide your vision,
And send our eyes to look for you on a mission.

What a pleasure to look at night,
At God's painted Heaven,
We all ponder and wonder at a beautiful sight,
Only the Angels are allowed to play in God's Kingdom.

The beautiful morning star in the east sky,
To welcome the new day,
Then the evening star in the west,
She waves goodnight
As the sun goes to rest.

The plough can be seen in the north,
But that group of stars do change their port,
I think they change to confuse us for sport.

Venus as we know is the star of love,
And she alone steers us on a course
Like a kin to Heaven above,
For when we have love, it's so divine,
You could swear all the stars were yours and mine.

So when we say,
"Twinkle, twinkle little star,
How I wonder what you are,"
Think about the words,
It does make us wonder,
What is beyond that wild, blue yonder.

We can play amongst the stars,
And build our way, and make some stairs,
I'm sure it's quite a blessing to be high above our cares,
It's all waiting there, for whoever is brave enough to dare
It makes no difference where you are,
You can wish upon a star.

27/10/08

The moon

You sit up there in your lonesome sky,
Watching us and the world all 'round you with your eye,
Sometimes we only see a small part of you,
I am sure that's when you're first new,
As the nights pass by, you let us see you in full view.

On a clear night when the clouds are few,
I often watch as you weave in and out,
In gold you're clouth,
Darting and hiding and playing a game,
When you are full, there is no doubt,
Nothing on earth compares to your face.

For you are full of wisdom and truths we don't have,
You have always hung in the sky, so loyal and steadfast,
Watching life come and go, and never regretting the past,
You must wonder at us mere humans,
As we are always planning and plotting,
Most times to no avail, that's why we wail,
It must be good to stare at us,
You probably think why all the fuss.

You make us look so very small,
And to reach you we will never be that tall,
So carry on sweet moon, continue to give us your light,
Lovers speak of you, as they hold each other tight,
And all seems well in Heaven, this blessed night.

EARLY MORNING SKY

Sky of early morning,
Coloured purple, pink and blue,
Light tinges of grey, blends true,
The forecast promises a sunny day
As pale purple and pink mingle,
Trees seem to stretch their arms to heaven,
Every great tree pure and single,
The voices of the early morn reach my ears,
The sheaves of corn in the fields
Rustle like golden spears,
All the birds sing their sweetest notes,
They sing of loving thoughts,
The bright sunlight struggles through
Pale mists of purple, pink and grey,
For us the promise of a new day,
Only God could paint the morning sky,
As the sun peeps at such an early hour
Maybe her light is shy.

An Irish blessing

I wish you not a path devoid of clouds
Nor a life on a bed of roses
Not that you not ever need regret
Nor that you shall never feel pain,
No that is not my wish for you,
When mountains must be climbed
And chasms are to be crossed
When hope can scarce shine through,
My wish for you in times of trial,
And in every hour of joy and pain
You may feel God close to you,
May you always have a friend
Worthy of that name
Who will defy the daily storms of life at your side,
And those that help you in times of sadness
That every gift God gave you
Grows along with you
And let you give the gift of joy
To all who care for you.